LIVING

Life

ON

Purpose

MONICA D. LLOYD

Living Life On Purpose

by, Monica Lloyd

Printed in the United States of America

ISBN 978-0983362715

Unless otherwise indicated, Bible quotations are taken from the King James Version.

DEDICATION

This book is dedicated to the living.

For as long as there is breathe in your body,

you have purpose to fulfill.

Welcome into your Glory.

ACKNOWLEDGEMENTS

To my Savior, Jesus Christ

Thanks for placing purpose within me.

If there were no You, there would be no me.

I will follow through and stay focused.

I would also like to acknowledge some very important people who are part of my journey.

Laura E. Robins, my mother. She was received in Glory in 1999, knowing that her purpose on earth was completed. She always stated that she was placed on earth to be a good mother and, after receiving salvation, "to give God all she got." She was known as a "Woman of Faith" and helped many leaders stay on the path, no matter how crooked the enemy made it seem.

Apostle Donald C. Ruff, my spiritual Father, who too was called into Glory in 2008. He was known as the "Apostle of Favor" and a great Man of Influence. When he spoke, everyone listened. He saw greatness in me that I never could have seen without his guidance, and he let me know,

"It's not about you." This helped me to develop Godly character and integrity, and for that I say, "Thanks you."

To **Apostle Dr. Sharon R. Ruff** (the wife of the late Apostle Ruff): Thank you. I am in awe and at a loss for words to let you know how much I greatly appreciate your shepherding and the love you have for the flock. The Lord definitely knew whom to place over his sheep at Word & Truth Church, a place of healing and deliverance. I will continue to follow my Naomi as I reach for the handful of purpose that you leave behind for me daily. God bless you.

Lloyd Family, George (husband), Cory, Louis, and Julian (my Kings in the making), I love you all very much. Thank you for your prayers and quiet times. To my husband: you are the wind beneath my wings. You push ever so gently, lifting me higher and higher, and for that I appreciate and respect the man you are. You are my King.

Cabrina Robins (my sister) thank you for your support and love. It's a blessing to have family that believes in your purpose and capabilities. You never doubted, and you shall reap the fruit thereof.

Word & Truth Church Family, We are People of Purpose, Called to Greatness, and Distinguished by the Anointing.

TABLE OF CONTENTS

FORWARD

My purpose was first revealed to me as I sat crying in my living room as I sought the Lord in an effort to understand some of the painful events and experiences that were occurring in my life. It was at that moment I heard the voice of God (through his Spirit) say; *you are The Standard of Holiness for Women."* From that day forward, I was on my way to understanding why I was here, to which "purpose" answers that question.

From the moment Elder Monica came into our ministry, her focus and mind-set has been on PURPOSE! As a woman, her heart felt desire is to live life on purpose, and she longs to see God's people discover their purpose as well. I have heard her speak on "purpose" in many venues and to whoever would listen as she expounded ON PURPOSE!

This book is a journey or a step-by-step means to help you not only understand purpose, but to help you find out how to discover and identify your God given purpose. Therefore, I challenge every one that reads this book to take heed to the wealth of knowledge that Elder Monica shares in this book, and pursue PURPOSE! For it is purpose, that will give meaning to a great portion of your struggles, pain, battles, failures and victories.

You must know this; God is a God of purpose, and he knows the purpose of every person that he allows to be born into the earth realm. Know this; if there was NO PURPOSE to your life YOU WOULD NOT BE HERE!

So, in closing, it is my prayer that everyone that reads this book enters into "purposeful living" which will cause you to reach your "predetermined" destiny. In Jesus Name I pray. Amen!

Apostle, Dr. Sharon R. Ruff
Senior Leader of Word & Truth Church
Founder/President of Sweet Rose of Sharon Women's
Ministry

PREFACE

A Message from the Author

(Before You Begin)

Fulfillment, according to Webster's Dictionary, means *to make full, to put into effect or bring into reality.* There is much needed in our land and you have the key. Your gifts and talents are the answers to many peoples' questions. God has made you full of purpose that is required to flow out of you for such a time as this.

I have often wondered and searched for a reason for my existence in life. In my growing-up years, it always seemed that I never fit into the scheme of things. I was what some would call a loner, not being alone, but I enjoyed being in my own company.

I often kept myself locked in my room, delving into some great book as I visualized with the scene that was unfolding. I loved reading novels. They provided me a place to travel beyond the circumstances by which I found myself surrounded.

The words that were expressed were captivating, and

they drew me into a place of safety and security where I was in control. I needed to be in control.

My parents separated when I was young, and this brought on some insecurity regarding my self-worth. In a child's eyes it appears that, they are the cause of one of the parents to leave. I loved my father and he meant the world to me. However, his departure tore something deep within my heart, and my perceptions of "fathers" left a negative taste in my mouth until I found out that the Lord tasted so good *(Psalms 34:8)*.

For me, finding the Lord was an exhilarating experience! I knew for the first time that this love was going to be secure, dependable, and unconditional with all of my issues. He restored and renewed my faith in fathers by removing all of the icicles from within and caused my tears to cleanse my soul.

I found a "new me." Misery or becoming someone's footstool never was God's plan, but to bring Glory to the King who set me free. In Him, I became a new creature, and all of my old things (self-pity, hatred, bitterness, resentment, manipulation, etc.) passed away, and behold I became new *(2 Corinthians 5:17)*.

I am a woman with a purpose, and God has a plan for my life. In Him, I move, breathe and have my being. I exist because of His love for me. I am prosperous because he says I am. I am someone to be reckon with and so are you. Hear the words spoken to Jeremiah:

"Then the word of the Lord came to me [Jeremiah], saying, Before I formed you in the womb I knew [and] approved of you [as My chosen instrument], and before you were born I separated and set you apart, consecrating you; [and] I appointed you as a prophet to the nations. Then said I, Ah, Lord God! Behold, I cannot speak, for I am only a youth But the Lord said to me, Say not, I am only a youth; for you shall go to all to whom I shall send you, and whatever I command you, you shall speak. Be not afraid of them [their faces], for I am with you to deliver you, says the Lord. Then the Lord put forth His hand and touched my mouth. And the Lord said to me, Behold, I have put My words in your mouth. See, I have this day appointed you to the oversight of the

nations and of the kingdoms to root out and pull down, to destroy and to overthrow, to build and to plant.

— Jeremiah 1:4-10 (AMP)

You were chosen from birth, separated and appointed to do all that the Lord has placed inside of you to do. No more shall you be tossed back and forth as someone aimlessly walking with no direction. He knows you and He has great plans for your life—plans that were created before your existence.

You are not a mistake as some may think, but a child who has purpose and a great future awaiting you. So find yourself in the will of the Lord and be a steward of the gifts that have been bestowed upon you. The things that you desire will become fruitful in their season. Just give yourself time and continue to move forward. Keep walking.

"But seek (aim at and strive after) first of all His kingdom and His righteousness (His way of doing and being right), and then all these things taken together will be given you besides." — Matthew 6:33

The Master holds you in the palm of His hand, always

watching and protecting His plans. He holds you tenderly, with much love and compassion, looking upon you with great expectation. Just follow through and stay focused, knowing that the Master will not allow you to fail, but He will see that you succeed.

We learn by trial and error, and this occurs only to keep us humble. We should never get to the point in our lives where we think that we don't need God. What a big mistake!

Inside of you is the Lord's DNA, and at the appointed time you will awaken from stupor and the world will be your enlarged territory. Tread upon it with excitement, knock on doors that are closed, keep your head held high and be not weary in well doing. You shall reap if you faint not *(Galatians 6:9).*

As you read this book I pray that you find yourself asking the Lord, "What must I do to bring you Glory?" The angels look upon man every day and ask God why is He so mindful of us. Mind the things of God and He will make sure that you taste the finer things in life. He has an expected, good end for you!

INTRODUCTION

From Bondage to Freedom

*When Pharaoh let the people go, God led them not by way of the land of the Philistines, although that was nearer; for God said, Lest the people change their **purpose** when they see war and return to Egypt. But God led the people around by way of the wilderness toward the Red Sea. — Exodus 13:17-18 (AMP)*

Have you ever set your mind to an endeavor, only to find out that there was more required than you originally thought? It's called "counting the cost." The children of Israel were in bondage four hundred years before Moses, their deliverer, came to set them free. All they knew was they wanted out.

God also knew their hearts and heard their cries just as He hears yours today. We make some outstanding promises to God, if He would only deliver us from our current circumstances:

"Lord, I promise I will never ..."

"Lord if you bring me out of this I will ..."

"Lord never, ever again will I do this....just help me out of this."

The Children of Israel were exactly that—children. They were not ready for battle. All they had ever known was hard work and labor. If they had known how to fight, they would have freed themselves years before, but fear had them captured and crying out to their God for deliverance.

God had a plan, and a man whom He was going to use to bring them out of bondage. He counted up the cost and had a roadmap for their journey. He protected them at the most delicate and tender part of their lives. The children had a father who set himself to be their shield and buckler. He is a caring God. In the midst of your journey, He will not let allow destruction to be your portion.

Children need protection and safety from the "big bad wolf" known as the devil, which produces a lot of wind when he talks. God knows how to protect us from the elements of life if we could ever learn to stay in the assigned secret place. Being out of the will of God removes us from safety in which the enemy has legal rights to eat us alive. Stay in your secret place.

The Israelites could have changed their purpose as soon as they saw danger and return to back to Egypt (bondage), the place that caused them much grief and disappointment, but God refused for that to be an option. He led them into another direction called the wilderness.

Jesus Christ, after fasting for 40 days, was led up into the wilderness to be tempted of the devil by the holy spirit on purpose *(Matthew 4:1)*. You may think that He was being set up to fail. Quite the contrary; he was being set up to conquer. A wilderness experience will allow many of your own selfish desires to die off and true Godly character will arise within your spirit. God wants to see more of Him in you.

Being in bondage, enslaved to something, is never pleasant. You have no freedom and someone is always pulling you backwards when you desire to move forward. You have dreams and plans, but none of them seems to come into fruition.

As a result, you become hopeless.

There is a greater future and an expected end awaiting you. Jeremiah 29:11 (NIV) states, *"For I know the plans I have for you," says the Lord. "They are plans for good and not for disaster, to give you a future and a hope."* The Israelites were in bondage a second time when God came and visited. God informed them to get comfortable and relax for at the designated time He will bring them out, again. When the timing is right release will come and they will move forward and become what they were destined to be from the beginning.

I felt like one of the children of Israel. I wanted deliverance, but wasn't mature enough for the promises. I wanted to be free, but had a loss direction. My equilibrium was off. I wondered within myself, "Why am I here? What is my purpose and what should I be doing?"

I repeated those questions daily. Until one day, the answer came in the midst of my worship, the Lord told me to start seeking His will and desires and surrender my own and He would establish my going. I needed to stay focused.

Before I could start, I needed to learn how to stop. Stop reacting to my surroundings and learn to act. Stop letting things and people dictate to me what I should or should not be for the Kingdom, but trust in Him who knows my future and holds my life in His hands. Depending on another was not optional, but believing in the leadership he placed in my path to lead the way was needful.

He had already purposed to bring the children of Israel into their promised land where they could multiply and be fruitful. The same goes for you. It is time for you to do the will of the Lord. You are ready to be about your Father's business for the kingdom.

Be encouraged and know that the paths you have taken were for a reason and were always leading somewhere. Stepping-stones make your feet steadier. This is not the time to turn back. You have traveled too far. Continue walking and do not rush, but be persistent. Make every step count.

The book, *A Purpose-Driven Life*, by Rick Warren has allowed many individuals to discover their purpose for life.

God uses us all in different capacities for Kingdom-Building.

For while one saith, I am of Paul; and another, I am of Apollos; are ye not carnal? Who then is Paul, and who is Apollos, but ministers by whom ye believed, even as the Lord gave to every man? I have planted, Apollos watered; but God gave the increase. — 1 Corinthians 3:4-6

I have a "feeders" anointing. I help build people up into the righteousness of God—setting them **right**, not **straight**. This is not bragging. This is how the Lord uses me for Kingdom Building. I love to eat naturally and he has empowered me to feed spiritually. How awesome is that?

First Corinthians 3:4-6 states: "*One plants and one waters, but it is God who provides the increase.*" No servant is an island; we are co-laborers in the Gospel. We each have our own assignments to carry out and complete. You stay in your lane and I will stay in mine.

Learn who you are to be in the Kingdom and work it. That calling will lead you to the treasures that are locked inside of you and will provide you with your own personal wealth.

Fruitfulness is required with purpose. You never want to do anything without seeing some productivity. For example, a bank will not give you a loan unless you can provide a business plan. They need to see what you see. The bank wants to know how you are going to make your business grow and what your short and long-term goals are.

I started many projects in my life without evaluating any outcomes and none of them was successful. Having passion is not enough; you have to have guidance and counsel. Place your vision before your eyes and count up the cost. Make time for it and find a mentor that has accomplished what you are seeking.

Where no counsel is, the people fall: but in the multitude of counselors there is safety.— Proverbs 11:14

On my Christian journey, I learned a lot about myself. I learned that I was selfish, self-centered and self-reliant. I only needed God when it was convenient for me. I was an independent woman who thought she had it all together and God did not always fit into the scheme of things.

Why should He? I felt I would be one of those children about whom He would never have to worry about, because "I got this." I did not want to be a bother to the Father. He has enough children that call on him daily. I forgot I am only a child in the Lord's eyes as well and I still needed him.

One day I came to realize that I was living a nightmare. Failing at everything, I wanted to accomplish, absolutely no progression, and finding my self-esteem getting lower. The spirit of doubt and confusion was taking over. This child found herself on her knees repenting and asking the Father for help. No longer was I miss independent, but became miss dependent. I make no move until I get in agreement with my Father, not him get in agreement with me.

I had to develop a humble and submissive spirit and learn to let the Holy Ghost be the guide for my life. I am bought with a price and much has been given for me to be a part of the Kingdom of God—the key words being, **"A PART,"** not an individual. There are no solo acts in the

Kingdom. We are the Body of Christ, and He is coming back for a bride (church) without any blemishes. I am part of the church and you are part of the church, therefore there is much work to be done.

If you were honest with yourself, you would admit that this is how you relate to God as well. As long as things are going well, you avoid consulting Him on anything. You feel you have it all figured out.

In all your ways know, recognize, and acknowledge Him and He will direct and make straight and plain your paths.
— Proverbs 3:6

Enjoy yourself while you are fulfilling your call, and step out on faith. You have to look beyond where you are now, and know that God already has everything prepared for you. Have a willing heart and an obedient spirit that will increase your appetite to eat the good of the land. Never think you are doing this alone. Your Father knows what is needed even before you start. Stay connected to Him, and you will never get lost on this journey.

Joshua and Caleb discovered in Jericho that there was

a land of abundance called, Jericho. It was there all of the time, waiting for them to find it. It is waiting for you in the great USA.

I pray that whatever parts of the world you may reside in that you become enlightened with clear vision, so that the Spirit of the living God will reveal His secrets to you concerning your region and provide instructions on how to fulfill purpose for the Kingdom.

The harvest truly is plenteous, but the laborers are few; Pray ye therefore the Lord of the harvest, that he will send forth laborers into his harvest. —Matthew 9:37-38

Purpose has been around since the beginning of time. It is not a new thing. It was with you as you were being formed in the womb of your mother. You are not an afterthought or a mistake. You were being created to be great.

You were chosen for such a time as this. God is getting ready to use you to show His power (strength), so that His name may be declared throughout all the earth. Are you up for the challenge?

Keep in mind that purpose is not about you, but God working through you to display his Glory. You cannot get prideful and think—as you are being used—that you are doing this on your own. The Glory will leave and you will be standing by yourself.

For no flesh shall glory in his presence. — *1 Corinthians 1:29*

Show the power of God in your life through your gifting and talents. Your purpose and passions work hand in hand—you cannot operate one without the other. They need each other.

God was passionate about returning us to good standing with him. Even after sin entered the Garden of Eden, He was willing to give His all and His best to make that return happen.

For God so greatly loved and dearly prized the world that He [even] gave His only begotten (unique) Son, so that whoever believes in (trusts in, clings to, relies on) Him shall not perish (come to destruction, be lost) but have eternal (everlasting) life. — *John 3:16 (AMP)*

Jesus carried out his Father's plans, plans that brought forth such excitement in the land that people are still talking about Him today. People tend to have short memories, so if they are still talking about our Savior there has to be some truth to it!

In the process of rewarding His Son for a wonderful service, He raised Jesus' name above all names and no one can come to God unless it's through Jesus Christ. What an awesome privilege! Servants get recognition!

That at the name of Jesus every knee should bow, of things in heaven, and things in earth, and things under the earth; — Philippians 2:10

As you go through this book, you will see PURPOSE in an acronym form:

P – Produce: To bring to fruition, to give birth to.

U – Understand: To get the meaning of a task.

R – Respond: The giving of an answer.

P – Plan: A method of accomplishing an assignment.

O – Optimism: Displaying a positive attitude.

S – Self-Control: Knowing yourself and how to control you.

E – Endurance: The ability to withstand hardship.

Purpose will provide all the things that are required for you to succeed. It will be a blessing to you naturally and spiritually. We serve a God who is concerned about the wholeness of humanity (mind, body and soul). He wants all of your needs met.

Following through on your purpose will bring you

wealth, and not necessarily money. A good peace of mind with contentment is wealth in abundance. People are losing their minds and doing some dangerous things to themselves and others. I like to say that their mind has slipped; slipped from believing in Christ, slipped from knowing right from wrong, and slipped right out of their body. It is okay to laugh.

Make purpose a fantastic experience and enjoy the journey Have you ever heard someone say, "You did that on purpose?" What they were referring to was that the individual put thought into their actions before activating it. Living life on purpose is living a planned life with thought put into it. It is having goals set for each day. It is saying I purposely want to succeed; therefore, this is what I will do to make this come into fruition. Go and be productive. It is in you.

PURPOSE

Hebrew Translation

yatsar[1]

(yä·tsar')

1) to form, fashion, frame

a) (Qal) to form, fashion

1) of human activity

2) of divine activity

a) of creation

1) of original creation

2) of individuals at conception

3) of Israel as a people

b) to frame, pre-ordain, plan

(fig. of divine) purpose of a situation)

Purpose is intentional. It is an aim or a goal.

LIVING LIFE ON PURPOSE

P – Produce

U – Understand

R – Respond

P – Plan

O – Optimism

S – Self-Control

E – Endurance

Purpose... What is it?

Why on earth are you here? That is the question on everybody's mind and as soon as you know the answer, everything else will fall into place in your life. You can probably then begin to understand all of the mess-ups, rejections, abuse and mental madness that you experienced along the way. Maybe, just maybe, you can find peace. All the things you have gone through have to mean something. If all things work together for your good, there was a purpose of good somewhere when you failed, felt rejected or were misunderstood.

Purpose was never meant to be complicated. There is an enemy in the land and his purpose and goal is that you never become enlightened, refreshed, renewed and know that you have been called into the Kingdom to fulfill the plans of the Lord. He is a thief and the Father of Lies - a shepherd that does not have your interest at heart. Never trust a word he says.

*The thief comes **only** in order to steal and kill and destroy. I came that they may have and enjoy life, and have* *it in abundance (to the full, till it overflows). — John 10:10, Amplified*

Take note of the word **"ONLY,"** meaning this is all he does: kill, steal and destroy. He is limited to only three things, whereas Jesus states that He came "that they may have life, enjoy life, and experience abundant life" to the fullest and until it overflows.

How awesome is that? He speaks of no death, not taking anything away from you or destroying anything in your life. He wants to give you a productive fruitful life, and serving a Lord like him sounds grand. What do you think?

Have you ever misplaced your keys and looked all over the place for them, only to find them right in front of your face? You might have even said, "If it was a snake, it would have bitten me," because those keys were so close. Your purpose is very close, and all it will take to discover it is for you to open your eyes.

I remember when I was going to nursing school and taking chemistry, which was one of the hardest subjects for me to comprehend. I could not get the concepts of the equations on my own no matter how hard I tried. A classmate of mine took notice of the difficulties I was having and gave me what he called a quick solution. He stated, "Monica everything has a pattern. Just follow the pattern."

I meditated on it and he was right. There was a pattern to every equation. If I discerned the pattern, I got the answer. I say to you, the greatest thing with which you find yourself struggling, there is a pattern. The answer for your deliverance is all wrapped up in it.

For example:

1. If you are having problems within your marriage, but you both agree that divorce is not an option, God could be preparing you both for marriage ministry. You may have discovered some good communication tips to strengthen a marriage.

2. Let's say your finances are in the basement. God can give you a creative idea that will bring you out of the hole and bless others as well. These ideas are called "witty inventions" *(Proverbs 8:12)*.

Wherever you find yourself at this moment, there is yet

purpose in your life. Look outside of yourself and see the Lord. Not your capabilities with your intellect, but with God's wisdom.

Purpose is doing the Father's business with passion.

And He said to them, how is it that you had to look for Me? Did you not see and know that it is necessary [as a duty] for Me to be in My Father's house and [occupied] about My Father's business? —Luke 2:49 (AMP)

Regarding the scripture above, Jesus knew at the age of twelve what He came to the earth to do and nothing could deter him from fulfilling that plan, not even death. He had a business to tend too. God has a business and he is hiring employees. Are you willing to work? The gifting He has placed on the inside of you from birth is to help Him accomplish all that is needful on earth, but he needs workers.

You are a predetermined individual with a bright future. You're not a joke or a clown to be laughed at. You are not an after-thought or a creation with which God does not know what to do. You now understand that God is calling you into greatness and the direction you should follow has been revealed to you. God orders your steps on purpose, and you have been ordained for an assignment.

This should give you confidence as you begin to move forward in doing Kingdom Business. God knows how He created you, and He knows your likes and dislikes more than you. Dismiss the enemy's thoughts when he tells you that doing business for the Kingdom is boring and that you will see no rewards. He lies.

Matthew 6:33 states that as you seek to do first things first, your Father will give (no payment required) to you the things you desire. Also, know that God is not a hard taskmaster. He works with what you have already displayed. Purpose is nothing new, but what you are currently doing. If it is cooking, continue to cook. If it is sewing, then create clothing that makes people look good. We do not want any naked kingdom people.

My purpose is to FEED. I love feeding people God's word. My passions are writing, speaking and reading. These three allow me to flow and I love doing them willingly. That is how much I know that my purpose can benefit the Kingdom of God. I feed men, women and children of all nationalities. God prepares my menu and I cook it and serve it up with my style.

My gift makes room for me to enter. I need not network or pass out business cards. If I continue to stay in my lane, the people that need what I possess will find me. Sick people find doctors. People with bad toothaches find dentists and pregnant women go to obstetricians. When individuals get hungry enough for the word of God, they find me and I feed them.

A man's gift maketh room for him, and bringeth him before great men. — Proverbs 18:16

I must not neglect my gift and think it is small and not beneficial. Just because I am not a genius does not mean I am worthless. We often belittle ourselves because we are not on the frontline. Be grateful that you are *in line,* and when the time comes for you to move up front, be ready and maximize the moment.

A gift is as a precious stone in the eyes of him that hath it: whithersoever it turneth, it prospereth. — Proverbs 17:8

God wants my purpose, to feed me too. Please do not think that you are working free. If He can take care of birds and lilies, he will take care of you. Worrying about provisions will hinder your progression. You must believe that God has supplied all you will need for this journey and he will get you there safely. This is not to say you will not experience any turbulence, but you will land safely.

Consider the lilies how they grow: they toil not, they spin not; and yet I say unto you, that Solomon in all his glory was not arrayed like one of these. If then God so clothe the grass, which is today in the field, and tomorrow is cast into the oven; how much more will he clothe you, O ye of little faith? And seek not ye what ye shall eat, or what ye shall drink, neither be ye of doubtful mind. For all these things do the nations of the world seek after: and your Father knoweth that ye have need of these things. But rather seek ye the kingdom of God; and all these things shall be added unto you. — Luke 12:27-31

Genesis chapter two speaks of four rivers; Pison (spring forth), Gihon (burst forth), Hiddekel (rapid waters), and Euphrates (sweet waters) with each river representing something distinctive. The reason in mentioning these rivers is that God wants rivers flowing out of you continually. He desires for you to be springing forth with new ideas and inventions. Bursting forth with new revelations, rapidly pursuing your dreams, and taste the sweetness of your success. Allow your rivers to flow. Have more than one stream of income. How about having four.

Wake up every morning and say, "How do I live on purpose today?" "What am I going to do on purpose to make my life better?" Have a plan for your day. Write it down before you lay your head on the pillow for the night and awake with fresh breath to accomplish at least one of your tasks, if not all.

Dr. Martin Luther King was a man of purpose. I have read his speeches and he was a great orator if there ever was one. His words could mesmerize a crowd and bring people hope when they felt hopeless. Provide vision when there was no vision left. Give dreams when the dreamers stopped dreaming. He was a man appointed for a designated time when the people needed a leader who could write the vision and make it plain.

I recall the looks in my parents' eyes when they would listen to him speak. It was a look of pride and self-respect. My father would sit there in his chair and turn the television up so that he could hear Dr. King clearly. My mom would stop whatever she was doing, come and sit down and hold me in her lap as we looked at a square box that showed a black and white picture with so much life coming through it. It was colorful to us.

Dr. King's "*I Have A Dream*" speech let us know that there is a promised land on earth, a land that is flowing with milk and honey. A land without violence where there can be peace in the midst of confusion. He saw even then, what we are experiencing today. How can you say that you are confused about -why you are here?

From his mouth to this page:

"In the process of gaining our rightful place we must not be guilty of wrongful deeds. Let us not seek to satisfy our thirst for freedom by drinking from the cup of bitterness and hatred. We must forever conduct our struggle on the high plane of dignity and discipline. We must not allow our creative protest to degenerate into physical violence. Again and again we must rise to the majestic heights of meeting physical force with soul force."— Dr. Martin Luther King Jr.

On his journey to destiny, Dr. King lived on purpose. He encountered many challenges and obstacles, but they did not detour him, stop him or push him backwards. He kept the momentum until his death. Purpose will sometime cost you your life and you have to be willing to pay the price. You have to believe in whom you serve and that He rightly sees your deeds unto Him.

Dr. King believed in equality for all men, and why not? Even the Declaration of Independence stated it:

"We hold these truths to be self-evident, that all men are created equal, that they are endowed by their Creator with

certain unalienable rights that among these are life, liberty and the pursuit of happiness."

Let's take a closer look at this:

"We hold these truths to be self-evident." *Without a shadow of doubt what we are about to say has been well proven.*

"That all men are created equal". *In the beginning, God (the creator) created the heaven and earth and in Genesis 2 He created male and female, equally. This eliminates any color or gender being more prominent than another.*

"They are endowed by their Creator with certain unalienable rights." *Therefore, being created by God, there are placed within them certain rights, special gifts and talents to be carried out, which are not to be separated from them or transferred to another.*

"That among these are life, liberty and the pursuit of happiness." *They are freely to pursue an abundant life with freedom and happiness. No bondage is to be placed on them.*

Now let's read our expanded version all together:

"Without a shadow of doubt what we are about to say has been well proven. In the beginning, God (the creator) created the Heavens and Earth, and in *Genesis 2* He created male and female, equally. This eliminates any color or gender from being more prominent than another. Therefore, being created by God, there are placed within them certain rights, special gifts and talents to be carried out, which are not to be separated from them or transferred to another. They are freely to pursue an abundant life with freedom and happiness. No bondage is to be placed on them."

The Declaration of Independence was adopted by the Continental Congress in 1776, announcing that the thirteen American colonies then at war with Great Britain were now independent states, and no longer a part of the British Empire. The birthday of the United States of America—Independence Day—is celebrated on July 4, the day the wording of the Declaration was approved by Congress.

The United States holds freedom for many people. It is unfortunate that so many of us who have been living here our entire lives haven't found out that this land flows with milk and honey, and that we have a right to the pursuit of happiness. We are still bound by our own limited mindsets without knowing how to enlarge our territory.

Living a full and effective life is within all of us. We have a mechanism that has been placed in us to succeed. No, it is not will power, but *God's* will, along with *His* power.

Kingdom Living is Purposeful

Life in the Kingdom is a place of security and dominion. It was designed for the citizens of God to dwell and live in abundance. Jesus stated in John 10:10 *"I am come that they might have life, and that they might have it more abundantly."* Take notice of the word 'might' for it is not a guarantee you will have the abundant life if you do not believe.

Have you ever wondered why you are not wealthy? Have you ever noticed in scripture the word **GIVE**?

"But thou shalt remember the LORD thy God: for it is he

that giveth thee power to get wealth, that he may establish his covenant which he sware unto thy fathers, as it is this day". ------*Deuteronomy 8:18*

The meaning of the word *GIVE* according www.dictionary.com is, *to hand to someone, to place in someone's care, to grant permission, opportunity, or to impart.* It is freely given unto you.

God has given (granted, placed in your care, handed to) YOU the POWER to get wealth. He is not going to give you the wealth, but the POWER to get it. He is a POWER-GIVING God. He wants you to pursue your wealthy place and He knows you are able to do it.

"But seek ye first the kingdom of God, and his righteousness; and all these things shall be added unto you." Matthew 6:33

Your requirements are to seek Him and accept his power; not things, but him; not His hand, but his face. Seek the ways of God and the power to get wealth will come. He will add it unto you. No work required.

Sitting down is not using the POWER

Dreaming only is not using the POWER

Being Slothful is not using the POWER

Put some movement in your feet, (not your mind) and watch where you will go. God desires to put His glory upon you so that your way can become prosperous. He is not of a selfish God. If you delight in Him, he will GIVE you the desires of your heart. *(Psalms 37:4)*

Many people have cheated themselves out of living because they think they cannot do any better. You have no vision for your life. There is so much potential on the inside you, but you allow fear to paralyze you. I refuse to die with potential on the inside of me. I want to die empty, completely empty of all the things God has placed on the inside. I want to be fruitful and productive for my future generations. It is called leaving a legacy behind, an inheritance for my children's children.

Living life in the Kingdom was purposed from the beginning. The Garden of Eden was a kingdom place. To be considered a kingdom three things are prevalent: a king, territory, and citizens. Adam was the king, the garden the territory, and Eve was the citizen. All three ingredients were in place.

When a good king loses his kingship, the people suffer and have to follow another. This is what happened to Adam. He lost his kingship to the adversary who caused mankind to fall subject to his antics, tactics, and way of life. Nevertheless, God had a redemptive plan to bring humanity back into the kingdom into their rightful position of authority.

Jesus the Christ bought us back from the ungodly king of this world with his blood and paid the price. He placed us back into the kingdom under his kingship with authority and power. He (Jesus) is the King of Kings, the earth is his territory, and the blood bought believers are the citizens. Jesus has a Kingdom.

The things that I do, I do for the Kingdom. I have what one may call, Kingdom Assignments. I am about my Father's Business. As I continue to fulfill my position and work with passion, the Father will pay accordingly. I trust him with my life and all my possessions. He is the one who gave them to me anyway.

The kingdom life is a lifestyle that has to be walked out daily. Your speech is not of those who do not believe, but of good news. You have a dialect of faith. The things you see your father do, that will you achieve and do.

"And Jesus went about all Galilee, teaching in their synagogues, and preaching the gospel of the kingdom, and healing all manner of disease among the people." ----- *Matthew 4:23*

Preaching is speaking and the gospel is good news. Living life in the kingdom requires both. Get back to kingdom living.

LIVING LIFE ON

P.U.R.P.O.S.E

PRODUCE

PRODUCE

When God has a purpose for your life, He expects you to be fruitful. You are not to remain dormant or go and bury what is in your hands. He is looking for a return on His investment. He is looking for fruit.

You came from a God who creates things. He produces or gives birth to things. He impregnates us with his Glory. When Mary (the mother of Jesus) had been promised in marriage to Joseph, before they came together, she was found to be pregnant [through the power] of the Holy Spirit (*Matthew 1:18).*

The scripture says that when he was born, the child (Jesus) grew and became strong in spirit *(Luke 1:80).* No father likes to see his child stunted, finding it hard to comprehend the requirements for progression and growth. That father will quickly find help or other resources in order for his child to succeed. His child must produce. So is it with your Spiritual Father in heaven.

Six times throughout the *Book of Genesis* it is stated,

"Be fruitful and multiply."

1.   *Genesis 1:22*

And God blessed them, saying, Be fruitful, and multiply, and fill the waters in the seas, and let fowl multiply in the earth.

2.   *Genesis 1:28*

And God blessed them, and God said unto them, Be fruitful, and multiply, and replenish the earth, and subdue it: and have dominion over the fish of the sea, and over the fowl of the air, and over every living thing that moveth upon the earth.

3.   *Genesis 8:17*

Bring forth with thee every living thing that is with thee, of all flesh, both of fowl, and of cattle, and of every creeping thing that creepeth upon the earth; that they may breed abundantly in the earth, and be fruitful, and multiply upon the earth.

4.   *Genesis 9:1*

And God blessed Noah and his sons, and said unto them, be fruitful, and multiply, and replenish the earth.

5.   *Genesis 9:7*

And you, be ye fruitful, and multiply; bring forth abundantly in the earth, and multiply therein.

6.   *Genesis 35:11*

And God said unto him, I am God Almighty: be fruitful and multiply; a nation and a company of nations shall be of thee, and kings shall come out of thy loins;

Every single time God made the statement "Fruitful and Multiply," His requirement was that you make it fruitful and produce more of it. He commanded you to "Be." *Be* like your heavenly Father. *Be* like a child called for greatness and *Be* all that you can be, with a trust in Him to make it all come to pass.

You are Kingdom-Builders. You have been given dominion and authority over everything according to *Genesis 1:28.* This earth belongs to God and his children. Rise up and take your rightful place. Don't bury the gifts that have been bestowed upon you from birth. Stir up the gift and use it.

For it is like a man who was about to take a long journey, and he called his servants together and entrusted them with his property. To one he gave five talents [probably about $5,000], to another, two, to another, one—to each in proportion to his own personal ability. Then he departed and left the country. He who had received the five talents went at once and traded with them, and he gained five talents more. And likewise he who had received the two talents—he also gained two talents more. But he who had received the one talent went and dug a hole in the ground and hid his master's money.—Matthew 25:14-18

The first two servants were demonstrators and because of their obedience and knowledge of their master, they were fruitful and multiplied. The master trusted that these servants observed how he did business and would do likewise. He did not tell them how to make it fruitful. The last servant went and buried his money. If you read *Matthew 25* further, you will find out that the lazy servant never made an attempt to do anything; therefore no fruit came forth from him.

Upon the master's return, he wanted each servant to give an account of what they did with the talents he had given to them. As you read above, the one with five talents went and made another two talents. The one with two talents went forth and made two more talents. The one with one talent did nothing, correction he buried it. God expects fruit from his children according to all that he has placed within us. This is not the time to say what you have is not important, for it is. Use it.

The master, after receiving the report, took the talent of the servant who did nothing and gave it to the one who started out with five for he knew this employee would produce even more. I guess you can say the lazy employee never received a promotion, but instead his master terminated him. Promotion comes from God, and God will not elevate lazy, procrastinating individuals. Is this you?

Are you able to produce what God has placed into your hands? A small beginning can produce a great harvest. What are you doing with it? Has anyone ever seen your gift? Is it still in the package, meaning your body, the temple, if so un-wrap it today for all to see. Let us have a coming-out party. Surprise!

No gift is insignificant and all gifts are needed. Here are three men to whom the master entrusted an amount of money. What I find amazing is that he distributed different amounts to each of them. He gave to them according to their own ability. It is good for employers to study their employees so they know who is equipped for a certain task. In any group of people, one will find motivators, agitators, impersonators and demonstrators.

A **Motivator** is an individual who has a team concept and is able to move the team forward with the vision that has been placed in front of them. He or she is the cheerleader and one that is an example for all to follow. Every team needs a motivator. They keep individuals uplifted when things are not looking its best, for their focus is on the prize and reaching the end together.

Jonathan, King Saul's son in *1st Samuel 18*, loved David like his own soul. He became so connected to David that he became a great motivator for him. King Saul tried on multiple occasions to kill David with no success. When there is a call along with purpose on your life, the enemy, to quote M.C. Hammer, "can't touch this."

Even though Jonathan was to be next on the throne, he saw the anointing on David and knew that God had purposefully handpicked him to become the next king over the children of Israel. Motivators see the big picture, not only what is in front of them.

An **Agitator** is one who rubs everybody the wrong way. He or she is the pessimist of the group and sees no possibility of productivity in the endeavor at hand. They like to stir up trouble and get reactions from others. They are the individuals from whom you turn away when they enter a room. God will utilize these individuals to expose what is in your heart. They help you fulfill purpose with style. They will hang themselves eventually or remove themself from the team.

Jesus shows us good leadership skills in His dealing with Judas. Here Jesus had someone on his team that he knew didn't understand the vision and someone who would eventually betray him. Judas's focus was, *"What about me?"* If you listen to agitators, they will often say, "What do I get out of the deal." "What's in it for me" or "they are always picking on me." It is me, me, and me. They never see how they are affecting the team, until it is too late. They are fired.

Then Judas, which had betrayed him, when he saw that he was condemned, repented himself, and brought again the thirty pieces of silver to the chief priests and elders, Saying, I have sinned in that I have betrayed the innocent blood. And they said, What is that to us? see thou to that. And he cast down the pieces of silver in the temple, and departed, and went and hanged himself. — Matthew 27:3-5

An **Impersonator** is a pretender. Impersonators like to imitate others, but are not sincere. The gift of discernment works well on these individuals. They can only keep up the pretense for a while; eventually their true colors will shine forth. Their momentum dies out.

Psychics, fortunetellers and witches are great examples of this. They work in a realm that is not of God, but is fed through their father, the devil. Our adversary had always wanted to be like God the Most High, which is the reason why he was kicked out of heaven *(Isaiah, chapter 12)*.

Impersonators admire the individuals they desire to become. They will take on those individuals' characters and try desperately to eventually replace them. Be cautious; they are not your friends. We are to emulate Christ, not impersonate Him.

A **Demonstrator** connects well with motivators. They are good listeners and doers. Their hearts are into what they do. These individuals can and will do what is required regardless of what others on the team may put forth. They have no problem in serving without any complaining. It is in them to do what is right. With a demonstrator, you can truly say they believe that they have a master of higher authority watching over them and their desire is to please Him. I like demonstrators for they can become demon busters.

Servants, be obedient to them that are your masters according to the flesh, with fear and trembling, in singleness of your heart, as unto Christ; Not with eye service, as men pleasers; but as the servants of Christ, doing the will of God from the heart; With good will doing service, as to the Lord, and not to men: Knowing that whatsoever good thing any man doeth, the same shall he receive of the Lord, whether he be bond or free. — Ephesians 6:8

Upon the master's return, all three servants had to give an account of what they did with his money, for he was a businessman. The scripture said he was gone a long time, which allowed them time to do something, to come up with something, but one servant went and buried his money.

Then he which had received the one talent came and said, Lord, I knew thee that thou art an hard man, reaping where thou hast not sown, and gathering where thou hast not strewn: "And I was afraid, and went and hid thy talent in the earth: lo, there thou hast that is thine. — Matthew 25:24-25

Fear = **F**alse **E**vidence **A**ppearing **R**eal. Fear will cripple you and cause you not to move. It will freeze you in place. The servant said he had fear. Fear of what—trying? Failures only lead to successes. Keep trying.

In order to be productive, you have to do an assessment of where you are now. If you have been doing a task and it hasn't progressed, here are two things you can do:

1.   Cut It Down – Stop doing it.

"And when he saw a fig tree in the way, he came to it, and found nothing thereon, but leaves only, and said unto it, Let no fruit grow on thee henceforward forever. And presently the fig tree withered away." — Matthew 21:19

If you have planted anything that has not produced, cut it down. Stop spinning your wheels in exhaustion, attempting to impose your will instead of God's will. Perhaps the timing and/or season were off. Not to say it won't come around again, but it is best to do it in God's good, acceptable and perfect will.

And be not conformed to this world: but be ye transformed by the renewing of your mind, that ye may prove what is that good, and acceptable, and perfect, will of God.— Romans 12:2

Once you try it again, when everything is in order and you have been spiritually released, then you will be firmly planted and bringing forth good fruit that will last. Maybe God needed to do some development within you.

"And he shall be like a tree planted by the rivers of water, that bringeth forth his fruit in his season; his leaf also shall not wither; and whatsoever he doeth shall prosper. —
Psalms 1:3

2.   Prune It – Get it in shape.

He cleanses and repeatedly prunes every branch that continues to bear fruit, to make it bear more and richer and more excellent fruit. — John 15:2 (b)

If you are producing even a little bit, hang on in there. God will come in and cut off the things that are hindering the process for growth. He will do some cleansing and deep washing. This is needed so that the fungus does not spread to the areas that are producing.

Pruning is not a pleasant process. It is painful, but the end results are glorious. Pruning requires cutting of the flesh and your heart. Since Jesus is the Master Surgeon, he knows exactly how to cut and even knows how deep to go. Whatever it takes, lift up your arms and say, "I surrender all."

Once the pruning process is completed, you will bring forth much richer and more excellent fruit. You are destined to feed many who are hungry for what God has purposed you for.

I was an individual who negated criticism. Therefore, seeking counseling was not a strong point of preference for me. I share this with you so that you can understand that in the multitude of counselors there is safety. There is safety from error, safety from wandering and safety from pitfalls.

Where no counsel is, the people fall: but in the multitude of counselors there is safety. — *Proverbs 11:14*

It is not that the Godly people whom you trust are trying to stop you; they are watching out for your soul. Watching you struggle is not easy for them to observe. I remember when I joined Word & Truth Church (W&TC) and Apostle Donald C. Ruff asked me, *"What do you want from this ministry?"* I quickly replied with my arrogant self, "To grow without any hindrances". In other words, let me do what I want to do.

I mentioned nothing about helping me to grow or getting me more developed in God's word. I thought I was doing his ministry a favor to be there. See I was already an Evangelist upon my arrival at W&TC and I thought I was working my purpose and gifting. I came to find out that I needed to be cut and deeply. I bled for six years under the profound leadership of Apostle Ruff with him being true to his name, RUFF.

I can truthfully say God knows exactly where to plant you in order to get purpose out of you. Today I am known as Elder Monica and Big Sister amongst the congregants. Much growth has come out of me and the character of God developed within me. I am no longer the same. Let God do what is necessary for your growth and stop running from correction. You don't want to be a bastard child.

But if ye be without chastisement, whereof all are partakers, then are ye bastards, and not sons. — Hebrews 12:8

One of my favorite scriptures is *Psalms 45:13*: *"The king's daughter is all glorious within."*

Glory never works from the outside in, but from the inside out. Let God place His Glory on you so you can produce. I am a daughter of the King and He has Sons. Kings leaves inheritances for their children and living a purposed-filled life will bring you to yours. Go and achieve yours. Living life on purpose knows that you will be successful.

LIVING LIFE ON

p.U.r.p.o.s.e

UNDERSTAND

UNDERSTAND

*The LORD looked down from heaven upon the children of men, to see if there were any that did **understand**, and seek God. — Psalms 14:2*

The word **UNDERSTAND** means *to comprehend a task or realize what must be done.* Let us say a manufacturer created a product and wanted to sell it, but no one knew how it worked. The only individual who knows the purpose of the item is the creator. God is your Creator; therefore, He knows what you are designed and purposed to do. Your requirement is to seek Him.

I have never seen a person start new employment without receiving a job description or a new gadget that comes without instructions. In each case, if things do not turn out right it is because neither party understood or comprehended what was required. The new person loses his or her job and the new gadget never gets used to its fullest potential.

My husband bought a new cell phone, which came in a box with three different booklets. His only concerns were calling and texting. His interest in internet usage, ring tones, down loading music was of no significance. He cared about only the two features that he knew how to operate.

As children of the King, you too have many features, but have you read or understood the manual—the Bible? Inside, it tells you what you possess and how to operate your potential to the fullest. Like the Ragu spaghetti, sauce commercial: "It is in there." You have great potential inside of you, for God placed it there at birth.

Understanding takes studying. Remember when you were in school; the teacher taught a lesson and would then say, "Go home and study. You will have a quiz on this soon." After studying what was originally taught, you developed an understanding. Doing the task became easy and you flowed without much opposition.

The Lord desires for you to study your gifts and learn how they flow, but the only way you can learn this is by studying your word, the Bible.

Study to shew thyself approved unto God, a workman that needeth not to be ashamed, rightly dividing the word of truth.— 2 Timothy 2:15

God is placing the responsibility of studying on you. He is not *(just like natural teachers)* going to make you do your lesson. You have to be mature enough to understand that in order to pass the test, you have had to study. No time allowed for distractions or procrastination.

Once you know what you were created for, you will be able to reach the world and be used to a greater capacity for the Kingdom. Not having an understanding limits your capabilities and your ability to fulfill the ultimate existence of your life. You will never be fulfilled until you do what you were created to do.

That is why it is so easy to blame others for your unhappiness. You expect people to fulfill you, when in reality God created you to be fulfilled in Him. It's not up to your mother, father, husband or children to make you happy. It is up to you to understand that purpose needs to be accomplished and you must start today. Make your steps in Him and allow Him to guide you along the way.

His purpose was for the nations to seek after God and perhaps feel their way toward him and find him—though he is not far from any one of us. For in him we live and move and exist. — Acts 17:27-28

Having an understanding of purpose allows you to pursue it with great intensity. The understanding will build your confidence and increase your momentum. A journey only becomes long when you do not know where you are going. Everyone needs direction, every now and then.

In the 12th chapter of Genesis, God told Abram to leave his country, relatives and father's house and go to a land that He would show him. Abram was going to a place where he had never traveled, in a direction he had never taken. I am quite sure it was taking him out of his comfort zone and that is a good place to be.

When you feel you have everything all figured out and believe you can handle it on your own, that is the best time for God to show up and let you know that you have been doing it wrong the entire time. You have to learn to stop and listen to the Creator, for He has things to share with you. Lean not to your own understanding and never trust your emotions. Emotions can change multiple times throughout the day. God does not operate on our emotions, but on our will to serve.

Trust in the LORD with all thine heart; and lean not unto thine own understanding. — Proverbs 3:5

Abram had to depend on God and trust in their relationship. He had to know that God knew what He was doing and, wherever that took him, they would go there together.

And I will make of you a great nation, and I will bless you [with abundant increase of favors] and make your name famous and distinguished, and you will be a blessing [dispensing good to others]. And I will bless those who bless you [who confer prosperity or happiness upon you] and curse him who curses or uses insolent language toward you; in you will all the families and kindred of the earth be blessed [and by you they will bless themselves]. So Abram departed, as the Lord had directed him. — Genesis 12: 2-4

God shared with Abram the plans He had for Abram's life. He told Abram his purpose. God would:

1.   Make him a great nation.

2.   Bless him with abundance

3.   Make his name famous and distinguished.

4.   Make him a blessing to others.

Abram was to be a blessing, and he could not fulfill purpose in his father's house. He had to get an understanding of that and start going in the direction in which God was leading. What is preventing you from fulfilling purpose?

The blessed assurance in knowing that God has purpose for you is also in knowing that God has a prepared place and destination for you as well. If you are willing, He will take you there—to a place that is flowing with milk and honey. Abram was willing and as Abraham he was known as the richest man in his country, all because he trusted God and understood his purpose of being a blessing.

..give me understanding and I shall live [give me discernment and comprehension and I shall not die]. — Psalms 119:144

Purpose commands you to live. Jesus Christ was all wrapped up in purpose. His birth was purposeful; being born of a virgin proves that. Now check that out. His purpose was so important and definite that God did not allow the sperm of a sinful man, by the name of Joseph, to interfere with His plans.

This is where God's character of *El Shaddai* came into operation, meaning that whatever does not exist to enable you to carry out the plans of the Lord, He will create for you. He is more than enough! There are no excuses with God, just results.

Mary, the mother of Jesus, was chosen to be the one to bring the Savior into the world. She accepted her assignment like a champion willing to carry it out. When the angel came to speak to her, she questioned the salutation (greeting) she received: *"Hail, thou that art highly favoured, the Lord is with thee: blessed art thou among women." (Luke 1:28)* and the scripture states she thought to herself.

She was troubled at his saying, and cast in her mind what manner of salutation this should be. — Luke 1:29

Mary needed clarification and understanding immediately, if God was going to get her to see what He had in store for her. Perceiving her thoughts, the angel answered her quickly.

And the angel said unto her, Fear not, Mary: for thou hast found favour with God. And, behold, thou shalt conceive in thy womb, and bring forth a son, and shalt call his name JESUS. He shall be great, and shall be called the Son of the Highest. — Luke 1:30-32

Notice that the angel lays out the plan, but doesn't say how this will all take place. How can a virgin have a child? It is medically impossible without a seed. Now I hope you can understand the scripture when it states that with man this is impossible, but with God ALL things are possible for there is nothing too hard for God to perform. He is *El Shaddai* (God of More than Enough) and if it needs to be created, He will do just that – create.

Then said Mary unto the angel, How shall this be, seeing I know not a man? And the angel answered and said unto her, The Holy Ghost shall come upon thee, and the power of the Highest shall overshadow thee: therefore also that holy thing which shall be born of thee shall be called the Son of God. -Luke 1:34-35

The creator opened Mary's womb to be receptive of what the spirit of God was capable of doing. She perceived it, conceived it, and received it. With Purpose, you have to see it believe in it and bring it to pass.

For three years, Jesus turned this world upside down and people are still talking about Him today. Martin Luther King, Jr. fulfilled purpose and went on to glory after saying, "For I have seen the promised land."

Have you ever looked at an individual and said within *"I wish I was like them?"* I have. I admire the ministries of many different people. I love Bishop Jakes, and I absolutely adore Pastor Jackie McCullough. In the past, I have heard them explain how God got them to what you see now. You see their Glory, but you may not know their stories.

Once (some many years ago) while sharing with other pastors, Bishop Jakes' wife Mrs. Serita Jakes said that you have to be careful whom you allow into your home. She would invite people over to their home in the beginning of their marriage and the furniture was not up to their expectation in the humble beginnings.; for example their couches were on crates. The following day, those same people would be talking about the condition of their home. I can promise you this; those same people are not talking now. I do not know why that (of all things spoken) stuck with me, but I understood afterwards.

I also interpreted for myself in the midst of her words that some people attach themselves to you for either positive reasons or destructive purposes. One will have to discern the intents of people's heart as you pursue your purpose, and it is okay not to take everybody, because everybody cannot go where you are going.

Bishop T. D. Jakes stated that he started in ministry with a small group of people not despising small beginnings, and God has blessed him with well over thousands and reaching more than that through media. People may not always found him attractive, but it never stopped him from preaching or opening his mouth to share the Good News. Just think if he had believed the report of people; we would not be hearing from a Bishop T.D. Jakes, the Father of Destiny (that is what I call him) say, "Get ready, get ready, get ready"; a slogan that got him on the map.

Purpose is not about you. It is about pleasing the Creator. Purpose is a building tool that God has placed inside you. Use it, and follow through on it with understanding in knowing this: you were chosen for such a time as this. Stay focused.

Each one of us has a road to travel and a lane in which to remain. The misunderstanding comes in to play when someone else's lane looks better or is moving faster than yours. Stay put; for your lane will become free flowing as soon as God removes the blockages ahead. Be patient, for it is a virtue. Go and achieve yours. Living life on purpose understands there is another day ahead.

LIVING LIFE ON

P.U.Rp.o.s.e

<u>RESPOND</u>

RESPOND

The uterus responds to the pressure that is placed on it. When a woman begins having contractions during her labor, the uterus begins to open up in order to bring forth new life into the world. It is getting ready to bring forth purpose.

According to Webster's dictionary, the word respond has two meanings:

To reply or answer in words.

To make a return by some action as if in an answer.

The first meaning requires you to open your mouth and give a verbal reply. Words need to come out of your mouth in order for the asker to hear that you understood the question with no nodding of the head or shrugging of the shoulders. Reply either yes or no. This is your time for letting God know if you are willing to submit and carry out the plans He has for your life.

A double minded individual will keep going in circles and the steps you take will always be confusing, leaving you wandering in the wilderness. Learn how to make sound decisions and stick to them. Let your "yea be yea" and your "nay be nay."

A double minded man is unstable in all his ways. — *James 1:8*

Ruth came from Moab, a place where Naomi's husband took her and their sons because of a famine in Bethlehem. When Naomi lost her husband and her sons in Moab, she decided to return to Bethlehem.

Ruth was Naomi's daughter-in-law, and she was determined to return to Bethlehem with Naomi. She knew this woman (her mother-in-law) had purpose on her life. She watched Naomi as she lost everything dear to her, and in the midst of it all, Naomi never cursed her God or lost her faith.

When Naomi tried to get Ruth to remain with her own people, Ruth responded with such profoundness. If God could find this kind of determination within you, there would be no limitation to what He could do through you. Ruth stated:

· "Your people will be my people."

· "You're God, my God."

· "Where you die, I will die."

By responding the way she did, Ruth was found by her husband Boaz and they had a child of the lineage of Jesus Christ, our Savior. Go read the *Book of Ruth* and you will see purpose throughout. Purpose will lead you to destiny and if single it will bring you before your mate.

Ruth had purposed in her heart that, no matter what, she was leaving a place of comfort and familiarity. These two things are what hinder most of you from moving forward. You are afraid of where you are going or what awaits you ahead. Therefore you say to yourself, "I will stay here," and you miss out on so much promise and adventure.

When God has revealed your purpose and His plans for your life to you, it is only polite to respond. Not with your head, but with your heart. Your response will move you closer to your destiny, because you have purposed it in your heart to do it God's way.

My heart has heard you say, "Come and talk with me."

*And my heart **respond**s, "Lord, I am coming. — Psalms 27:8*

The Disciples had to respond to Jesus as he called them to follow him.

As He was walking by the Sea of Galilee, He noticed two brothers, Simon who is called Peter and Andrew his brother, throwing a dragnet into the sea, for they were fishermen. And He said to them, Come after Me [as disciples--letting Me be your Guide], follow Me, and I will make you fishers of men! At once they left their nets and became His disciples [sided with His party and followed Him]. — Matthew 4:18-20

Notice their response: **"At once they left their nets and became his disciples."** They did not hesitate nor did they ask a whole lot of questions, but they dropped what they were doing and followed. They could have kept on fishing and going about their own merry ways, but they took a chance on the Savior and their lives were no longer the same. Jesus gave them a purpose-filled life. What about you? Connecting with a person who has purpose will lead you to your purpose.

When you have accepted your calling and told the Lord that you will go and fulfill purpose according to His standards, do your part in a manner that will be pleasing unto Him. Take your purpose seriously.

Your purpose is placed in your hands and how you make it grow depends on you staying connected to the Creator.

To prove to you that responses are very important, in reading *1st Kings 3rd chapter*, God said to Solomon, *"Ask what I shall give thee."* and Solomon replied, *"I am but a child; I know not how to go out (begin) or come in (finish)... Give your servant an understanding mind and a hearing heart to judge your people that I may discern between good and bad."*

An understanding mind and a hearing heart are awesome characteristics to have in purpose. You have to understand what you are responding to and learn to hear God with your heart. Look beyond yourself and see what God is really calling you to. Purpose is greater than you think. It looks to the natural eye like the tip of an iceberg, but in reality, the glacier is lying underneath.

Solomon knew that it took more than a call to be a good ruler. It took character, wisdom and knowledge to guide a people to their purpose. God loved Solomon's response; *"And the speech pleased the LORD, that Solomon had asked this thing"* (*1st Kings 3:10*). He gave Solomon what he asked for and the things he requested not.

God said to him, because you have asked this and have not asked for long life or for riches, nor for the lives of your enemies, but have asked for yourself understanding to recognize what is just and right, Behold, I have done as you asked. I have given you a wise, discerning mind, so that no one before you was your equal, nor shall any arise after you equal to you. I have also given you what you have not asked, both riches and honor, so that there shall not be any among the kings equal to you all your days. — 1st Kings 3:11-13

The Lord is calling people just like you to awaken from your sleep and realize that you are not living in a dream, for dreams only come true when you wake up. He is your light in the midst of darkness for He provides direction and the course of your life. When He calls, respond and stay focused on your journey.

Awake thou that sleepest, and arise from the dead, and Christ shall give thee light. — Ephesians 5:14

When God calls you answer, for if you do not the following word coming out of His mouth may be "NEXT," and this is not including you, and it will not mean Next Time. God is ever evolving and creating, and He is requiring workers who are willing to work. He will not ask you to do anything that He himself has not accomplished first.

In Genesis the first chapter you read how God created and over in the second chapter verse two you read this, *"And on the seventh day God ended his **WORK** which he had made; and he rested on the seventh day from all his **WORK** which he had made"*. God ended His work and rested from work. There is no need for rest if you have not done the work. What are you doing with purpose?

When my husband asked me to marry him, I replied with a resounding "YES." I loved him greatly and I was ready to get out of my mother's house. When God asks you a question and you do not respond, you are letting him know that you are not ready. You like where you are and are not willing to move. You will never leave the house without answering the person in charge of the house. Living life on purpose requires you to converse with the one who gave it to you. Open your mouth and respond.

LIVING LIFE ON

P.U.R.P.O.S.E

<u>PLAN</u>

PLAN

God is a planner and a creator.

In the beginning God created the heaven and the earth. —
Genesis 1:1

Genesis is a book of purpose and plans. It starts out by
telling you that God created the heavens and the earth. No
one gets credit but God. He had the blueprint and knew
how He wanted it to look. As you continue to read the first
chapter, you will see that He started in an order.

The earth was void and in darkness. No form or shape did it
have. It was just there. It is clear that no one can do
anything in the dark, but God had a plan.

And the earth was without form, and void; and darkness
was upon the face of the deep. And the <u>Spirit of God moved</u>
upon the face of the waters. — Genesis 1:2

The human body water weight is approximately 50% –
55% of water; depending on age, sex, height, and weight
(*<u>www.medindia.net</u>*), and you came from the earth. It is
going to take the Spirit of God to move upon your waters as
He provides his plans for your life. You became a living soul

once God breathed into your nostrils; until then you were not living, but existing.

And the LORD God formed man of the dust of the ground, and breathed into his nostrils the breath of life; and man became a living soul. — *Genesis 2:7*

You were created to bring forth the Glory of the Lord, and He planned well to get you to this point. In the Garden of Eden, God prepared all nutrients that would be needed before He brought any kind of life forth. Why invite people to eat if there is no meal? It is called planning.

On the first day, He created light, because it was dark. Light brings illumination. Whenever there is darkness in your life, shine light in it. The word of God is the light to chase away all darkness.

I am come a light into the world, that whosoever believeth on me should not abide in darkness. — *John 12:46*

Anything worth pursuing, and being successful, will require planning. You can become a great business man/woman if you do the work ahead of time and count up the cost. Do a business plan for your life. Where do you see yourself five years from now? Do you have a vision for your life? It takes vision to plan and a plan to have vision. They both work hand in hand. Where there is no vision, your life will cease.

Good planning and hard work lead to prosperity, but hasty shortcuts lead to poverty. — Proverbs 21:5 (NLT)

Jesus even stated in *Luke 2:49*, "I must be about my Father's business." Building the Kingdom is a business, and God has hired you way in advance. He is expecting you to be fruitful and train others in the purposes and plans of the Lord.

What kind of work are you doing? Do you recall why you were hired? If not, get reconnected to the Father so that He can give you your job description. You have PURPOSE!

Mr. Barak Obama did not become President of the United States (twice) over night (as some suppose). He planned. His political highlights are these:

1997 – 2004 — State Legislator

Obama was elected to the <u>Illinois Senate</u> in 1996, succeeding

State Senator <u>Alice Palmer</u> as Senator from Illinois' 13th District, which included Chicago South Side neighborhoods from <u>Hyde Park-Kenwood</u> south to <u>South Shore</u> and west to <u>Chicago Lawn</u>.

2004 — U. S. Senate Campaign

In May 2002, Obama commissioned a poll to assess his prospects in a 2004 U.S. Senate race; he created a campaign committee, began raising funds and allied with political media consultant <u>David Axelrod</u> by August 2002, and formally announced his candidacy in January 2003.

2005 – 2008 — U.S. Senator

Obama was sworn in as a senator on January 4, 2005, the fifth African American Senator in U.S. history and the third to have been <u>popularly elected</u>. He was the only Senate member of the <u>Congressional Black Caucus</u>.

2008 — Presidential Campaign

On February 10, 2007, Obama announced his candidacy for President of the United States in front of the <u>Old State Capitol</u> building in <u>Springfield</u>, Illinois.

Presidency

The *inauguration of Barack Obama as the 44th President,*
and Joe Biden as Vice President, took place on January 20,
2009.

From 1997 to 2009 were twelve years of development.
Now can you see that this was a planned adventure.
President Obama had a great business plan and I am quite
sure he didn't share it with everyone. Who needs naysayers
when you have vision?

The Lord walked on this earth for three and a half years
and ran a successful business that is still blessing people
today. Why? Because He had good workers in whom He
trusted and whom He had trained very well. He had a plan.
He picked twelve men, His Disciples, who turned this world
upside down.

Have you been divinely connected with individuals who
could set you on course and mentor you? Jesus mentored
those Disciples. He let them know the ins and outs of what
He expected. He lived a life in front of them and answered
any questions that came up. The Lord was teaching them

how a business should run. For example: pay your taxes.

However, in order not to give offense and cause them to stumble [that is, to cause them to judge unfavorably and unjustly] go down to the sea and throw in a hook. Take the first fish that comes up, and when you open its mouth you will find there a shekel. Take it and give it to them to <u>pay the temple tax</u> for Me and for yourself. — *Matthew 17:27*

Do the footwork and all else that is required of you. Walk out your plans after you have written the vision and made it plain for all to read. *(Habakkuk 2:2)* Create a blueprint. Look at it and see if it's workable. That is why people create business plans. Those plans help them to see long-term, as well as short-term, goals.

A majority of people cannot get a loan because they have no plan. Show me what you're working with and maybe I can bless you. Let me see what you see, saith the bank.

A man's mind plans his way, but the Lord directs his steps and makes them sure. — *Proverbs 16:9*

You may not have your whole future mapped out; in

fact, you might be overwhelmed if you knew up front everything God has planned! You simply need to be obedient and begin to do the things you know to do. God will be faithful and reveal more specifics along the way.

Roll your works upon the Lord [commit and trust them wholly to Him; He will cause your thoughts to become agreeable to His will], and so shall your plans be established and succeed. — Proverbs 16:3

Please do not think that the Lord isn't mindful of your desires and that He wants to control you. This is not the case. What He does know about us is that we can become self-willed and not include Him in anything we do, especially if we have the means to do it. Never make God an option; make Him the only choice.

Purpose is placed in your life to get you from one destination to another. How well do you think you can accomplish that without planning? Many mistakes are made because of lack of planning. Bad decisions along with consequences are displayed because of no planning. And a non-productive life will exist without purpose because there was no plan.

When I go grocery shopping, I have to make a list because if I do not, I buy everything under the sun. Then when I get to the register, I find myself over budgeted. It is so embracing placing items back because I over-spent. My desires got in the way.

Delight thyself also in the LORD: and he shall give thee the desires of thine heart. — Psalms 37:4

This can be considered an ambiguous statement. The Lord says if you delight yourself in Him, He will give you the desires of your heart. I always thought if I make the Lord happy, He would give me everything I want. All I have to do is to make Him happy, right?

It also could have meant that if I delight the Lord He will give (plant) special desires (His will) in my heart. This will allow me to be prosperous as I carry out the will and plans of the Lord. He would not plant things contrary to my personality for He knows what I like. I trust Him. Give the Lord all of you and watch what you will become: a vessel of honor ready for the Master's use. Planning is a recipe for success.

The children of Israel's victories were because of planning. Nowhere did you read about them waking up and saying, "I think I will fight today – Charge." It takes strategic moves to be in place in order to win battles. There are seasons of war. King David got into trouble with Bathsheba because he was not at war during his season *(2nd Samuel 11)* which caused him not to be purposeful. Joshua, with the battle of Jericho, was very fruitful in his season in bringing down the walls, and it was all because of a plan. God gave the instructions and Joshua followed the plan. Planning will bring miracles of success. Write it out and run with it.

In all thy ways acknowledge him, and he shall direct thy paths.---Proverbs 3:6

During the courtship phases the couple is planning how their relationship will go. Is there a future in this? Can you see yourself with me, forever? Will we get married? These are some questions asked, and if the both of them agree, the next step may be marriage, and a wedding requires planning.

Planning does not just involve one person; it involves people. Whatever you are planning at this moment I promise you it will affect someone else and because people are so unpredictable you may need to have a couple of plans in place. Just know this, planning will allow you to see the outcome of the vision. Go and achieve yours. Living life on purpose with a plan allows for few errors and disappointments. Plan accordingly.

LIVING LIFE ON

P.U.R.P.O.S.E

OPTIMISM

OPTIMISM

Optimism is the tendency to take the most hopeful or cheerful view of matters—to expect the best outcome. I have been told that it is your attitude that will determine your altitude. Positive people seem to have fewer physical ailments than those who are pessimistic (expecting the worst).

A negative attitude is not acceptable while fulfilling purpose. You have to know that God is mindful of you and wants you to be successful. He is not setting you up to fail. You have been chosen to do your assignment.

You can never let your circumstances in life dictate how you are going to feel or how you will react. Learn how to ACT and not REACT. Many jails are full of people who have reacted and are now living out their consequences. Regardless of how the day starts out or what the day looks like, it can always become better, stay focused, and know that you are not alone.

Lift up your heads, O ye gates; and be ye lifted up, ye everlasting doors; and the King of glory shall come in. Who is this King of glory? The LORD strong and mighty, the LORD mighty in battle. Lift up your heads, O ye gates; even lift them up, ye everlasting doors; and the King of glory shall come in. Who is this King of glory? The LORD of hosts, he is the King of glory. — *Psalms 24:7-10*

Before you give a presentation, it is not wise to say to yourself, "They are not going to like it" or speak any deadly words to your spirit. Death and life are in the power of the tongue and you shall reap what you speak *(Proverbs 18:21).*

There was a woman in the Bible who had a disease for twelve long years. She visited many physicians and they had not found a cure. One day, just as Jesus was passing by, " *she said <u>within</u> herself, If I may but touch his garment, <u>I shall be whole.</u>" (Matthew 9:21)*

The woman spoke to herself before touching the Messiah. She said "within" herself, if I can get to him, I know I can be made whole or well. No negative words came out of her mouth and she had what she spoke.

You have probably surrounded yourself with people who have allowed this world to take away their hopes and dreams and their speech indicates this. If you continue to be amongst naysayers or dream-killers, their attitudes will eventually consume you and your speech will become their speech. Disassociate yourself now while you have a chance.

Do not be so deceived and misled! Evil companionships (communion, associations) corrupt and deprave good manners and morals and character.

— 1 Corinthians 15:33

Let your words be pleasing to the One who has called you. You cannot repeat everything you hear. Especially if it is not in agreement with God's word. Speak only those things that have been revealed in your spirit. Know your Creator's voice.

Let the words of my mouth, and the meditation of my heart, be acceptable in thy sight, O LORD, my strength, and my redeemer. — Psalms 19:14

In today's economy, people's hearts are failing them from fear, but as a believer, you know that the Lord has not given us a spirit of fear, but of love, power and of sound mind. Our trust is in the Lord, not in this world system.

You are a child of the Kingdom of God, and there is always hope in our God.

*And **hope maketh not ashamed**; because the love of God is shed abroad in our hearts by the Holy Ghost which is given unto us.— Romans 5:5*

All the preaching, teaching, healing and deliverance that our Lord Jesus did while on the earth, He did with a positive attitude. He knew who He was and who sent Him, which allowed Him to work and fulfill purpose with authority and power. That same authority was passed on to you. Use it.

Learn to have the mind of Christ and you will succeed at everything you do. Have a compassionate heart and an open mind. Remember, you are doing the work of Him who has sent you, and you must be willing.

Your attitude displays much about your character. I was speaking one day and thought I did a great job. My message was "Get Rid of the "WO" and "Man UP." Teaching women that there is no need to cry, "Woe is me" if you know who you are in Christ. Who *He* is allows me to be is who *I* am.

After coming from the pulpit that day, the Lord was talking to my pastor about me. He informed her that I had much Attitude in my presentation more than the Anointing. My body gestures were to loose and my hand movements to abrupt. Boy, was my heart hurt! I thought I had related the teaching very well, and the women understood. I had received great compliments about the word of God that had been spoken and was assured that they had a better understanding.

Because I am not one to sulk long, and I repent quickly, I asked the Lord for clarification. I share with you what was released to me:

"When you are sent on an assignment, your desire should be for people to change, and it takes an Anointing to bring about change, not an attitude."

In other words, it is the Anointing that removes the yoke (bondage) from people. Yes, you do need attitude, but that of humility and not one of arrogance. Jesus did display the attitude of making corrections and setting people right and it all was done in love. I suggest that while you are fulfilling purpose, have a good attitude and be optimistic about all you do.

Stay focused, and don't allow anyone to get you off your square or push your buttons. Optimism, along with the joy of the Lord being your strength, will push you into a momentum that will carry you above the negative criticism of the haters in your life. Instead of merely believing you can fly, you will fly. Get excited about your future and make it all it can be. Go and achieve yours. Living life on purpose will carry you through the times of un-pleasantness as you move toward perfection in Christ.

LIVING LIFE ON

P.U.R.P.O.S.E

<u>SELF-CONTROL</u>

SELF-CONTROL

But the fruit of the [Holy] Spirit [the work which His presence within accomplishes] is love, joy (gladness), peace, patience (an even temper, forbearance), kindness, goodness (benevolence), faithfulness, gentleness (meekness, humility), self-control (self-restraint, continence). Against such things there is no law [that can bring a charge]. — Galatians 5:22-23

In order to fulfill purpose, you have to have self-control. Most people are failing in this area. They have not fully developed this fruit and, as with all fruit, you have to eat it so that it can get inside of you. Please take note that it is part of the fruit of the Spirit. Without the Spirit of God, there can be no manifestation of Godly self-control.

There are also fruits of the flesh. A lifestyle that, if lived outside of God's will and fulfilled in your will, becomes consumed by cheap sex (sexual immorality), lovelessness, trinket gods, paranoid loneliness, cutthroat competition, a brutal temper (which leads to abuse), divided homes and divided lives.

Fulfilling purpose requires that you allow the Spirit of God to lead you and be your guide. You cannot be Spirit-led children if you are not Spirit filled. *"Then was Jesus **led** up of the **Spirit** into the wilderness .... — Matthew 4:1*

*For as many as are **led** by the **Spirit** of God, they are the sons of God.* — Romans 8:14

Self-control is going to require that you walk it out on a daily basis. It is not about your own personal desires. You will have to learn the words "Yes," "No," and "I will get back with you," very well. For when you have purposed it in your heart to do things God's way, your enemy is going to do all he can to stop you. He will even work through people who are close to you. Divide and conquer is his mode of operation.

Learn to control your own spirit, and do not allow people and circumstances to get you off course. The Holy Spirit is a gentle and not forced on you. That would be called spiritual rape.

From your soul come your emotions and desires. If you

have no control over them, you will continually be tossed back and forth. Your feelings can change multiple times throughout the day, which may cause you to seem unstable. An unstable person cannot receive anything of value for his or her life. Having no self-control will cause people to wonder if you might have a mental illness, like bi-polar; up one minute and down the next. You can not have a see-saw mind set.

Whoever has no rule over his own spirit is like a city broken down, without walls.— Proverbs 25:28

This world is out of control, but God is still in control and nothing catches Him off guard. God does not tamper with your will, and whatever comes your way that may cause you to stumble or even fall, He (God) saw it in advance and prepared an escape.

Purpose is so important that you have to stay on course. Jesus did much in His three years of ministry, and He knew His job when He came to the earth. His whole story was told from Genesis to Revelation. He was written about throughout the pages of the Bible. He traveled through forty-two generations to become our deliverer from sin.

"So all the generations from Abraham to David are fourteen generations; and from David until the carrying away into Babylon are fourteen generations; and from the carrying away into Babylon unto Christ are fourteen generations."

— Matthew 1:17

Jesus' purpose on earth was to come and die (talk about having self-control!). He did not try to get out of His assignment or refuse it. He came and did all that was spoken of Him in the Bible. It was prophesied that He would fulfill His purpose. God's only begotten son would do what was required of Him, even unto death.

For God so loved the world, that he gave his only begotten Son, that whosoever believeth in him should not perish, but have everlasting life. — John 3:16

Building self-control will help you build Godly character. Here are some ways in which you can benefit:

- It increases self-esteem and confidence.

- It keeps you from becoming self-destructive and exhibiting compulsive behavior.

- It makes you a responsible and trustworthy person.

- It eliminates feeling helpless and hopeless.

- It gives you assurance of peace of mind.

I believe the reason why so many individuals are in debt is that they lack self-control, exhibiting no patience and no direction for their lives. They live paycheck to pay check, with their money already spent before they get it in hand. This vicious cycle has to stop.

We are purposed to live an abundant life according to *John 10:10*: *"The thief's purpose is to steal and kill and destroy. My purpose is to give them a rich and satisfying life."*

If you look closer at the scripture above, you will take notice that it says that "The thief's purpose." Thieves have purpose, but the Lord's purpose is to give us a rich, satisfying and fulfilled life. Many people are not satisfied and desire to be gratified to remove their pain, which causes dullness in the soul. It opens a door for thieves to come through and rob them of their joy.

Self-control is the key when it comes to purpose. No matter how good someone else's field may look, you must know that you are in the right field and vow to work your field until it produces fruit. The grass isn't always greener on the other side.

I must share this with you. I was clearing up my credit and was told not to apply for anything or open up any new credit for the next six months. If I did, I would cancel out the contract. I thought, *Wow this is going to be hard for me,* but I was ultimately successful.

Not giving in to my desire for instant gratification has now allowed me a new start in life. I have learned that "NO" is not a curse word, but a self-control mechanism. I can truly say being anxious for nothing is okay; in due season I will reap, if I faint not.

If this society works on a credit score, so be it. Give to Caesar what is Caesar's and give to God what belongs to God.

Now tell us what you think about this: Is it right to pay taxes to Caesar or not?" But Jesus knew their evil motives. "You hypocrites!" he said. "Why are you trying to trap me? Here, show me the coin used for the tax." When they handed him a Roman coin, he asked, "Whose picture and title are stamped on it?" "Caesar's," they replied. "Well, then," he said, "give to Caesar what belongs to Caesar, and give to God what belongs to God. — Matthew 22:17-21 (NLT)

I will do what is required by the law to remain in good standing in this worldly kingdom in order to be an example in a Godly Kingdom. Many Christians' credit is—in modern phrasing— "jacked up," for they believe Jesus paid it all and favor will make a way. Well, Jesus did pay for our souls to be redeemed back to the Father, but not for our credit. Although favor is not fair and is given to whomever the Lord desires, living on favor isn't fair to God.

When it was tax-paying season, Jesus paid what was due. He didn't tell the people, "I am your Messiah and you should be paying Me." He told his disciple to go to the brook, open the mouth of the first fish you catch, pull out the money and pay the taxes *(Matthew 17:27)*. Jesus followed the law of the land.

It is the law of this land that an excellent credit score gets you further than a poor one. How do you think an Oprah Winfrey can shut down ALL of Michigan Avenue to have her show and pay the bill in two days with cash if she didn't have excellent credit and self-control?

The best thing you have is your name. If you mess up your name (credit), you will not be trusted and no man will lend to you. The Bible says we are lenders and not borrowers. Having self-control concerning your life and money matters will lead you to a prosperous destiny.

Once you know your purpose and are walking it out, you will not be so quick to have you reputation scarred. You will do what is needed so as not to embarrass the Lord who has made your pathways straight.

What you have started, learn to complete. This is also self-control. Stop all the mini-projects and finish something. Jesus finished his ministry and left twelve disciples to continue it. What is it that you need to pick up again and complete? Go get it and do it.

You can't leave your purpose floating in the wind. People are waiting for you and they cannot get what they need until you get there. Rise up and walk. It is time. Don't violate or take for granted what has been established in you. Get in position and work in the lane you have been assigned. This too requires self-control.

Nothing is more frustrating than believing that you can do a project better than someone else and when the opportunity presents itself, you do not take advantage of it or you fail at it because it was not as easy as it appears. Self-control comes in when you do not place your own opinions into a matter in which you do not have all the facts.

One of the main killers of self-control is pride. Pride will always make you think that you can handle anything, do anything and not listen to anyone in the process. This can cause you to have a mighty fall.

"First pride, then the crash - the bigger the ego, the harder the fall."

— *Proverbs 16:18 (MSG)*

Keep your eye singled and keep your heart on track for this will allow you to follow through on your purpose and stay focused. You have charge of your attitude and you will decide which way to react on matters. Some people like to get a "rise" out of you; they live for it. See, if you are the individual whom everyone approaches to dump all their garbage on, it may be because they like seeing you as miserable as they are since you take things to heart.

Have you ever been told something about a person's problem and you wind up trying to figure it out for them? I used to be that way. I thought I was being helpful. All the while, I was making myself frustrated and upset while they were still repeating the same mistake, and it appeared they loved it. It is also called Co-Dependency.

One day I woke up and made a positive decision to STOP interfering in grown folks' lives and allowing myself to be a hindrance to their development. The only individuals that I am purposed to nurture are my three sons: Cory, Louis and Julian. I am their mother. I am my husband's helpmeet, and I will do that — help him meet what is needed in our home and with him.

I have to remain healthy in all aspects of my life in order to give my best to my family. I will not allow people to drain me or make me their way of escape. The Lord has already made a way of escape, if people only take it.

Don't become a crutch for anyone. Let people learn to lean on the Lord and not you. Yes, it feels good to be needed, but being needed is different from being available.

Being available is saying, "If I can help, I'm here"; whereas being needed is saying, "You can't make a move without me. You need me to carry you," and this is not good for either individual.

Hold your head up and look unto the hills from where your help comes, for it comes from the Lord (Psalms 121:1). Be encouraged in all you do.

I love to see people in different roles out of their comfort zone. How they handle it will reveal much about their character and how they control themselves. A leader, if they observe, will see how well they work at it or let it fall to the ground. Self-control (if it is matured) will attempt to try a new task and make it flourish. They will not pout, but water what has been placed in their hands. Self –control is discipline under control. Work at it. Go and achieve yours. Living life on purpose by having control over yourself will prevent you from becoming overwhelmed. Manage yourself first, before you have a business.

LIVING LIFE ON

P.U.R.P.O.S.E

<u>Endurance</u>

ENDURANCE

Endurance is the ability to withstand hardship. If you are going to fulfill purpose, you will have to learn to continue against adversities. You have been enlisted in the army of the Lord.

Take [with me] your share of the hardships and suffering [which you are called to endure] as a good (first-class) soldier of Christ Jesus. No soldier when in service gets entangled in the enterprises of [civilian] life; his aim is to satisfy and please the one who enlisted him.— 2nd Timothy 2:3-4

The cares of this world will destroy you if you let it. You have to stay focused and remember your assignment. Soldiers have to be alert at all times, if not; they can cause injury to themselves and their platoons. There are more than you at stake. Purpose is beyond you; therefore enlarge your forward and peripheral vision. Get a panoramic view.

There was a disciple in the Bible, by the name of Paul, who suffered much persecution and jail time for his belief in Christ. He considered himself a prisoner of Jesus Christ and for the Gentiles. He was willing to endure hardship for the benefits of others. Paul's education and magnificent speaking skills, along with his exceptional writing style meant nothing to him. It was about him giving Jesus Christ to the lost. Fulfilling purpose allows others to be free as you set the standard.

Whatever you have found your purpose to be, the process will involve many people to get you to your destiny, even your enemies. Judas, one of Jesus Christ's disciples, was the enemy to get him to the cross. Everyone needs at least one enemy to get him or her to purpose. . Be thankful for your enemies, for they are a sign that you are on course. Just stay focused.

History is a branch of knowledge dealing with past events and if knowledge is power, grabbing strength and endurance from our ancestors should push us forward, not backward. History has taught me that trouble will disappear; that this too shall pass and weeping does endure for a night when joy is coming in the morning. All I have to do is get through the night.

Endurance tells you to hang on in there till your change

comes. You are stronger than you think, for God has placed within you a mechanism to be an "over-comer" through all things.

Jesus endured what He went through on the cross *(being spit on, pierced in the side, nails in his hands and feet, and a crown of thorns on his head)* in order to place mankind back in right standing with God. He did nothing to get this kind of treatment, but it was purpose that made Him stay on that cross. He sacrificed His life to open up a gate through which others freely could come. Whosoever will, let him come.

The word **"Quit"** is nowhere to be found in the Bible. You are not a quitter, but a conqueror through Jesus Christ. The JOY of the Lord is your strength *(Nehemiah 8:10)*. Never think you can fulfill purpose on your strength.

One thing I have found out is that doing anything in your own strength will wear you out. I tried to do ministry with my own creative mind-set and found myself failing in every endeavor. Some things did get off the ground, but was not fruitful.

Eventually I surrendered my will to the Lord, and He told me to "Let It Go." He meant everything, and I did exactly that. I am fulfilling the vision of my home church as God continues to teach me to walk out what He has called me to be, which is a Teacher of Righteousness and Purpose. And I am not doing it in my own strength. Hallelujah!

To pick a profession and then make a decision to go to school and finish will take endurance on your part. The classes will become harder and you will have to study. The course may take years to complete, but you have to endure for the latter is greater than the beginning.

Fight the good fight of faith and finish your course. God is at the finish line waiting for you. Yes, there will be obstacles on your journey, but it is for your making. Keep the momentum and do not die out. People lose hope quickly if things are not progressing, as they desire. Let's go ahead and get this out of the way: nothing worthwhile is easy, but it pays off!

One of the happiest days of my life was when I received my Registered Nurse degree. I had worked hard for it. I had teachers tell me that I would never be a nurse, but I used those words not only to prove them wrong, but also to provide me with momentum and perseverance. Death and life are in the power of the tongue according to *Proverbs 18:21* and I was not going to allow negative words to destroy my dream.

Love...beareth all things, believeth all things, hopeth all things, endureth all things. — *1st Corinthians 13:7*

After his death, Jesus Christ rose on the third day with all power in His hands, and He transferred that power to us. We are the winners! There is no failure in God. You are only allowed three days to sulk in disappointment. Then you too must rise and try it again. Keep the endurance.

What will help your endurance is passion. If you love what you do you will do it sick and well. It becomes a part of your very being, and it is with you always. No one has to beg you to do it for you will do it freely. You can actually do it with your eyes closed. It does not become a burden, but a pleasure. Endure what you love doing.

Raising children requires endurance. Going to a job you

do not like takes endurance. Dealing with a spouse who is unemployed is endurance. We have it, but we choose on how we use it. Start using your to be effective in the Kingdom. It takes time to build a thing that will last forever. Rome was not built in a day and neither were you. It took nine months for your development within the womb, and your mother endured the nausea, vomiting, back pain, cravings, unable to sleep and unable to see her feet in order to get you here. Now God is asking of you to endure the vision, ministry, people, and purpose that he has placed within you. Bring it to fruition and present it to the world. You are more than able. Go and achieve yours. Living life on purpose with endurance will remove your eyes from people.

P.U.R.P.O.S.E

POWER POINTS

P.U.R.P.O.S.E. POWER POINTS

In Greek, the word POWER is EXOSIA or DYNAMI (Dynamite). It is an explosive BOOM! It is a word that demands change. The power of God living inside of you is demanding change. One cannot encounter the Savior and remain the same. To stay focused on this journey you must realize that you have power to accomplish all that has been placed within you. You are chosen for such a time as this to impact the world with power. What are you going to do about it?

In order to stay focused you have to imagine, or literally draw, a target in front you. There is a bull's eye right in the middle of the board and darts are thrown at it. The enemy uses fiery darts to try and stop you all the time, but your shield of faith kicks in and the darts' fire is quenched and are of no effect *(Ephesians 6:16)*. Aim purposely and you will hit your target.

Purpose is all about Kingdom-Building.

While Jesus did ministry, he never made himself the focal point. He always pointed to the Father. You will cease from doing Kingdom-Building when you find yourself pointing to yourself. Don't worry about recognition or rewards. God will reward you in your due season.

*And let us not be weary in well doing: for in **due** season we shall reap, if we faint not. — Galatians 6:9*

Purpose will bless those who are connected to you.

The children of God are the answer for the world today and the earth is in waiting for the manifestation of God's children to step up in power and dominion *(Romans 8:19)*. There are people waiting for you, and because of the assignment on your life, they are stuck until you step on the scene. That is why it is so vitally important that you stay on course. Lot was blessed because of Abraham *(Genesis 18th)*, Ruth was blessed because of Naomi *(Book of Ruth)*, and we are blessed because of Christ. Finish your purpose.

Purpose provides the F.O.G (Favor of God) on your life.

When driving through a fogged atmosphere,

people experience reduced visibility and a sense of being lost. They proceed with caution as they move toward their destination. Having the favor of God on your life allows you to proceed with confidence and surety, knowing that God is leading, and you must trust Him to make the way clear. Fulfilling the task at hand is not tedious, but joyous. The favor of God adds flavor to your life. It opens doors that would be closed and closes doors that you need not enter. I recall my mom saying, "Favor is not fair," and that statement proved many times to be true. Many things in your life were not deserved, but God saw fit to bless you with them anyway. That is favor: receiving undeserved benefits.

Purpose will bring out the haters on your journey.

Look at your enemies in a different light, for they are placed in your path to bring out the greatness within you. They are pushing you into your destiny all the while revealing to you the things that God is requiring for you to release self-pity, jealousy, revengeful attitude and self-will. Judas was the only one qualified (purposed) to get

Jesus to the cross. What enemy is helping you get to your cross?

Purpose adds "super" to your natural abilities.

I once heard a pastor state that God told her that He had given her grace to the tenth degree. Why? So she can do Kingdom Business. She went on to say that it would require the grace of God for her to accomplish that business. If God adds "super" to your "natural" it is because: 1) you need it, and 2) the assignment at hand will be more productive and fruitful with it. It is not about you showing strength; it is about showing God's glory. The reason many people get tired of doing ministry or their assignments is that they are doing it in their own strength. One needs to learn how to do their assignments through Christ Jesus and not through your own minor capabilities. (Matthew 16:19) The Lord wants to help. Let Him.

"YES WE CAN"

President Barak Obama had an awesome slogan while running for the presidency. It simply stated, "Yes We Can." People have for so long been saying what they can't do that they forgot about what they can do. Yes you can change; yes you can be fruitful; yes you can succeed; yes you can get a job; yes you can raise your children alone; yes you can; yes you can; YES YOU CAN!

You can even fulfill purpose all for the glory of God as you continue to seek the will of the Lord. Yes, you do have a purpose. Yes, there is a greater life in store for you and yes, you will stay focused. No more sidebar conversations, no more detours and definitely no more procrastination. We are now living in our DO and DUE season.

DO get up and start walking into the things of God. DO know you are called into a greater work for the Kingdom, and DO not give the enemy any mercy or a foothold into your life. He does not belong there. For in DUE season you shall reap if you faint not *(Galatians 6:9)*. Tell the devil, "SATAN YOU ARE A LIAR AND YOUR REQUEST IS DENIED!"

It is DUE you to prosper at this time, in this land where you dwell, but you will not be able to if you DO not pursue. The word "DO" is a verb, an action word, and it requires you to do something. The "DUE" is a reward word if you DO. Many of you have been fulfilling purpose and staying focused. You know your calling into the kingdom, and you have been working it. Now God is going to release your DUE (reward) for you have been faithful, and you did not give up. You do not serve a God who does not know how to pay His servants. He is a good rewarder to those who diligently seek Him *(Hebrews 11:6)*.

So once again, YES YOU CAN! Make it personal. We can, and we did, get a black man into the White House twice whom we believe will make a change (hopefully for the greater good) for the world. Moreover, there is a God who is also saying, "Yes We Can," as the children of the Kingdom rise up and take their rightful position.

When the righteous are in authority, the people rejoice: but when the wicked beareth rule, the people mourn (Proverbs 29:2).

Purpose has been around from the beginning of time—a

predetermined, understood revelation, purposely ordained, self-sufficient endeavor put in place by God. The world was formed for purpose and you were created for purpose. The assignment that God has planned for you has to be revealed to you. Stop asking everybody else what you are supposed to be doing. Why not ask God? He is the creator.

BREAK EVERY CHAIN

There is a song by Tasha Cobb titled, "There is power in the name of Jesus" and I absolutely find it liberating and refreshing. I hear within my spirit the words "BREAK EVERY CHAIN" so that purpose can be fulfilled here on earth as it is in heaven; whatsoever you bind on earth will be bound in heaven and what you loose on earth will be loosed in heaven *(Matthew 16:19)*. There must be freedom for there to be movement. People cannot walk freely being chained for it limits their un-limitless potential.

According to www.dictionary.com **break** means, *to smash, split, or divide into parts violently*, and life can do this to an individual. That is why it is so important to live life on purpose through Christ.

Get tired of being beat up. Get tired of being walked over. Get tired of being tired, because until you do your deliverance is still a distance away from you. Your purpose is waiting on you not the other way around. There is power in the name of Jesus!

How do you achieve Purpose?

- Break every chain of Rejection

- Break every chain of Slothfulness

- Break every chain of Low Self-Esteem

- Break every chain of Poverty

- Break every chain of Molestation

- Break every chain of Un-Forgiveness

- Break every chain of Pride

- Break every chain of Pornography

- Break every chain of Adultery

- Break every chain of Lack of Motivation

- Break every chain of Gossip

- Break every chain of Lying

- Break every chain of Slander

- Break every chain Cheating

- Break every chain of Back biting

- Break every chain of Wicked Imaginations

- Break every chain of being a False Witness

Let go of all of this. You are hindering your progression. The more you hold on to it, you will never reach your full potential for the Kingdom.

"Your future depends on many things, but mostly on you"
Author Unknown

A Prayer for your Release

Father God in the name of Jesus Christ our Lord, I break every chain that is prohibiting your people to move with swiftness and accuracy. Where the enemy has set up snares and traps I remove them from their path so that they do not stumble or fall. Let your people walk upright and focused on the desires you have placed within their hearts. Make them fruitful and multiply their endeavors for the glory of the kingdom. Touch and heal their Souls, and remove all calluses that have taken possession of their heart. Give them again a heart of flesh that is able to feel you once again.

Thank you for hearing my prayer, and require of them to write the vision and make it plain, in Jesus name I pray. Amen

P.U.R.P.O.S.E. NOTES

_____

_____

_____

_____

_____

_____

_____

_____

_____

_____

_____

_____

_____

_____

_____

_____

_____

_____

_____

_____

_____

REFERENCES

Bible Dictionary. (1978, 1999). Nashville, TN: Thomas Nelson Inc.

Publisher

Maxwell, John and Elmore, T. (2002, 2007). *The Maxwell Leadership Bible, 2nd Edition* Nashville, TN: Thomas Nelson Inc. Publisher

Wikipedia. *Barak, Obama.*

http://en.wikipedia.org/wiki/Barack_Obama

http://www.bible-history.com/eastons/E/Euphrates/

ABOUT THE AUTHOR

Elder Monica Lloyd is a woman with a *"Teaching Anointing,"* bringing about clarity of God's Word to the Body of Christ. She is purposed to feed those who are willing to eat. As Jesus asked Peter; *"lovest thou me"* and his reply was *"yes,"* Elder Monica's response is the same as she follows the instructions then given, *"Feed My Sheep."* Being in ministry for many years, she has discovered that serving others is a pleasure and is needful for growth. Leaving selfish desires along with self-willed ambitions allows for maturity in the things of Jesus Christ.

Elder Monica (as she is affectionately called) by the congregation of Word & Truth Church, serves under the Senior Leadership of Apostle Sharon R. Ruff. Elder Monica is the Director of New Member Classes, Director of the Hospitality Committee and a member of the Board of Church Elders. She believes being planted in the right church home will develop believers into Kingdom Builders. Elder Monica also serves as Board of Director for Sweet Rose of Sharon Women's Ministry. A ministry determined to teach, train, strengthen and support women while bringing about healing and restoration through the Word of God to women everywhere.

Elder Monica uses her first ministry; that of Evangelism to

share with others, that having a relationship with Jesus Christ will bring about a change and brings out the *"New Man"* described in II Corinthians 5:17 No one can come to Christ and expect to be the same!

Elder Monica is the wife of a loving and supportive husband of 26 years, Elder George Lloyd and the mother of two wonderful sons, Cory & Louis. She is an anointed speaker, has written several articles, newsletters, etc.

Her motto for life is *"God has a plan and that plan she will follow."*

CONTACT INFORMATION

Monica Lloyd
P.O. Box 1042
Dolton, IL. 60419
eswceo@yahoo.com
Facebook: Monica Lloyd
Twitter: @eldermonicadedication

www.ingramcontent.com/pod-product-compliance
Lightning Source LLC
LaVergne TN
LVHW021504080426
835509LV00018B/2399